INVASIVE SPECIES

CANE TOADS

by Martha London

FOCUS
READERS®

NAVIGATOR

WWW.FOCUSREADERS.COM

Focus Readers is distributed by North Star Editions:
sales@northstareditions.com | 888-417-0195

Produced for Focus Readers by Red Line Editorial.

Content Consultant: Steve A. Johnson, Associate Professor of Wildlife Ecology & Conservation at the University of Florida

Photographs ©: Shutterstock Images, cover, 1, 4–5, 7, 9 (cane toad), 10–11, 13, 19, 21, 27, 29; Pixabay, 9 (background); Red Line Editorial, 15; Brian Cassey/AP Images, 16–17, 22–23; Joe Raedle/Getty Images News/Getty Images, 25

Library of Congress Cataloging-in-Publication Data
Names: London, Martha, author.
Title: Cane toads / by Martha London.
Description: Lake Elmo, MN : Focus Readers, [2022] | Series: Invasive species | Includes index. | Audience: Grades 4-6
Identifiers: LCCN 2021003758 (print) | LCCN 2021003759 (ebook) | ISBN 9781644938553 (hardcover) | ISBN 9781644939017 (paperback) | ISBN 9781644939475 (ebook) | ISBN 9781644939888 (pdf)
Subjects: LCSH: Bufo marinus--Juvenile literature. | Introduced amphibians--Juvenile literature. | Pest introduction--Juvenile literature. | Nature--Effect of human beings on--Juvenile literature.
Classification: LCC QL668.E227 L66 2022 (print) | LCC QL668.E227 (ebook) | DDC 597.8/72--dc23
LC record available at https://lccn.loc.gov/2021003758
LC ebook record available at https://lccn.loc.gov/2021003759

Printed in the United States of America
Mankato, MN
082021

ABOUT THE AUTHOR

Martha London is a writer and educator in Minnesota. She spent much of her childhood picking up frogs and toads, but none were as big as a cane toad.

TABLE OF CONTENTS

CHAPTER 1

POISON TOAD LUNCH

The sun shines down on a river in northern Australia. A goanna basks in the heat. This large lizard is looking for its next meal. It spots a cane toad nearby. The lizard moves toward the brown, bumpy toad. Then it eats the toad whole.

The goanna quickly becomes sick. First, the lizard's heart starts beating

Monitors are large lizards found in Oceania, Southeast Asia, and sub-Saharan Africa. In Australia, people call these lizards *goannas*.

much faster. Next, the lizard loses control of its body. Then, its heart stops working. Finally, the lizard dies. The toad was its last meal. That's because cane toads are poisonous. Their poison has killed thousands of native lizards across Australia.

Cane toads are dangerous to more than just lizards. They have changed **ecosystems** in many parts of Australia. People have also brought this invasive **species** to other areas in the world. However, Australia has the world's largest problems with cane toads. By 2020, the toads had spread across 386,000 square miles (1 million sq km) of the country.

A cane toad's call is a series of low, quick sounds. People have compared it to the sound of a distant tractor.

Many scientists believe that the cane toad is one of the worst invasive species on the planet.

UNDER THE SKIN

Cane toads are poisonous for their whole lives. Even their eggs and tadpoles contain poison. This poison runs throughout their bodies, including in their organs. Cane toads also have two big **glands** on their shoulders. These glands produce large amounts of poison. The poison is a thick, white liquid. The toads use it against predators. They release the poison through their skin.

Cane toad poison can make animals lose control of their bodies. It can also be deadly. The poison can cause heart attacks. It can kill some animals in just minutes. A few people have died, too. But that's because they chose to eat parts of cane toads. The toad's poison is not a danger to most people.

PARTS OF A CANE TOAD

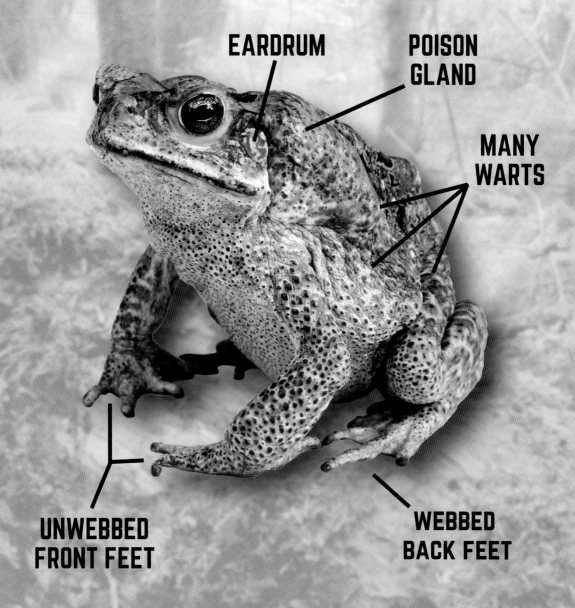

EARDRUM

POISON GLAND

MANY WARTS

UNWEBBED FRONT FEET

WEBBED BACK FEET

CHAPTER 2

ISLAND-HOPPING

Cane toads are native to Central and South America. Their range stretches through parts of Mexico. It reaches the southern tip of Texas. It also includes the island-nation Trinidad and Tobago.

In places where cane toads are native, other animals have **adapted**. For example, some predators are not harmed by the

Cane toads mainly get water through the skin on their bellies. That's why they often live in very wet areas.

toads' poison. Many animals do not eat the toads at all. Other animals eat the safer parts of cane toads. Those predators avoid the poison that way. As a result, cane toads do not kill off their native predators. Those animals are able to control cane toad numbers.

By the mid-1800s, people were bringing cane toads to new areas. For example, people brought the toads from South America to the Caribbean. In 1844, people took cane toads to Jamaica. They hoped the toads would get rid of rats there. However, rat numbers stayed high.

People thought cane toads could help with other pests. In the 1920s, sugarcane

The broad-snouted caiman is a natural predator of cane toads.

farmers brought the toads to Puerto Rico. The farmers wanted to get rid of a certain kind of beetle. These beetles killed sugarcane plants. After cane toads arrived, the beetle population shrank. So, people thought cane toads had helped.

For this reason, people took the toads to Hawaii and Australia in the 1930s.

Cane toads did not help farmers in these places. Even so, people continued to take cane toads throughout the Pacific, including to the Philippines and Papua New Guinea.

Cane toads have also ended up in Florida. In the 1950s, people started

SWEET-TOOTH BEETLES

British colonists first settled in Australia in 1788. They brought sugarcane with them. For decades, colonists tried to grow this non-native plant. Native Australian beetles caused huge problems. Their babies ate the roots of sugarcane. Farmers hoped cane toads would eat the beetle babies. The toads ate nearly everything. But they did not eat the beetles.

keeping cane toads as pets. Some of these toads escaped. By the 2010s, cane toads lived in the wild across much of southern Florida.

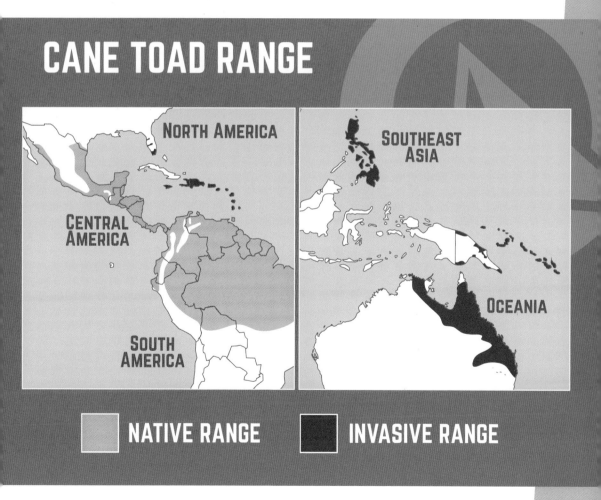

CANE TOAD RANGE

NORTH AMERICA

CENTRAL AMERICA

SOUTH AMERICA

SOUTHEAST ASIA

OCEANIA

NATIVE RANGE

INVASIVE RANGE

CHAPTER 3

BRINGING IN DISASTER

People often bring plants and animals to new areas. These non-native species are not always invasive. Some can live alongside native species. However, cane toads have caused serious harm to native species. For this reason, the toads are invasive in many places outside of their native range.

As of 2020, Australia was home to more than two billion cane toads.

Cane toads harm new areas for several reasons. One reason is that cane toads reproduce rapidly. A single female toad can lay up to 30,000 eggs at a time. In contrast, Australia's native frogs lay only 1,000 to 2,000 eggs at a time. In addition, cane toads grow up quickly. In warm areas, baby cane toads reach their adult size in only one year.

In areas such as Australia, cane toads also have few natural predators. No animals are there to stop the toads' fast breeding. For these reasons, cane toads often take over new areas. When that happens, the toads change native **food webs**.

Giant barred frogs are native to Australia. People often confuse them with cane toads.

Cane toads kill off the few animals that do eat them. Native snakes die because of cane toad poison. Monitor lizards die, too. In the late 2000s, cane toads spread to a new area in Australia. Scientists counted monitor lizard numbers in that area. After five years, approximately half of the lizards had died.

Scientists also found that crimson finch populations went up. Monitor lizards eat these birds. When the lizards died, more finches survived. This discovery showed how much food webs

LONGER LEGS

In the 2000s, scientists learned that cane toads were spreading across Australia much faster than before. The scientists found that cane toad bodies were changing over time. Some toads had longer legs than others. Toads with longer legs can travel more quickly. That's why they were spreading faster.

Crimson finches can be found across northern Australia and southern New Guinea.

are connected. One change can cause another change. That shift can lead to other shifts. As a result, invasive species such as cane toads can affect food webs in many ways.

CHAPTER 4

HERE TO STAY

As of 2020, people did not have a way to get rid of cane toads. Scientists believed cane toads were here to stay. But scientists still worked to control toad populations. Their methods tried to limit the toads' spread to new areas.

Removing cane toads is one control method. Scientists believe people should

In 2009, towns in Queensland, Australia, held the first Toad Day Out. People catch thousands of cane toads for the event each year.

focus on eggs and adults. Baby cane toads often look similar to native frogs. For this reason, baby cane toads can be difficult to find.

Many people catch adult toads by hand. Groups go out at night. They use flashlights to spot the toads. Then they grab them. The activity is known as

STAYING SAFE

Cane toads can be dangerous for pets. Dogs can become sick or die if they bite a toad. Children must be careful, too. They should never try to put cane toads in their mouths. People should also wear gloves if they pick up a cane toad. If they do not use gloves, they must wash their hands right away.

A professional toad remover catches a cane toad while toad-busting in West Palm Beach, Florida, in 2019.

toad-busting. People often catch huge numbers of toads in one night.

In some areas, toad numbers quickly bounce back. But in 2020, scientists learned that toad-busting may work in southeastern Australia. This area tends to be cooler. So, fewer toads travel there. Southern areas also contain more **isolated** groups of toads. As a result, those toad populations are less likely to grow back.

People also use traps to catch cane toads. One trap has worked especially well. The trap uses a light to draw in insects. These bugs are food for the toads. The trap uses a speaker, too. The speaker plays the calls of male cane toads. These calls draw female toads to the trap. Once caught, people kill the toads without causing them extra harm. The traps have become popular in Australia. In 2020, scientists showed they could also work well in Florida.

A string of cane toad eggs runs along the ground.

Getting rid of eggs is sometimes easier than removing adult toads. That's because female toads lay their eggs in strings. A jelly-like substance connects the eggs together. The toads often lay eggs in ponds and creeks. People can search these areas for strings of toad eggs. Then they can remove the eggs. In Australia, female cane toads tend to lay eggs twice per year. So, people know when to collect them.

Scientists are also studying how to protect native animals. Some study **taste aversion**. In the 2010s, scientists tested out this idea. First, they made sausages out of cane toads. Then, they put a chemical in the sausages. Next, they went to an area that cane toads had not yet reached. It was only a matter of time. In Australia, the toads spread approximately 30 miles (48 km) each year.

Scientists fed the sausages to native lizards. The chemical made the lizards sick. But the lizards recovered. They also learned. When cane toads arrived a few

Scientists were able to teach some blue-tongued lizards not to eat cane toads in the wild.

months later, the scientists tracked the lizards. The lizards that had eaten the sausages survived. These animals had learned to avoid eating the cane toads.

This method provided some hope. It could not control cane toads by itself. But it showed that **creative** ideas were needed. Scientists will keep finding new ways to keep native ecosystems healthy.

FOCUS ON
CANE TOADS

Write your answers on a separate piece of paper.

1. Write a sentence that describes the main ideas of Chapter 4.

2. What possible benefits and problems should people think about before bringing a plant or animal to a new area?

3. Which place has the worst problem with cane toads?
    - **A.** Australia
    - **B.** Florida
    - **C.** Mexico

4. Why are cane toads dangerous to their predators?
    - **A.** Cane toads often attack and eat their predators.
    - **B.** Predators that eat cane toads often become sick and die.
    - **C.** Cane toads rarely die when attacked by predators.

Answer key on page 32.

GLOSSARY

adapted
Changed over time to deal with a certain situation.

creative
Related to using the imagination, often to come up with new ideas.

ecosystems
Communities of living things and how they interact with their surrounding environments.

food webs
The feeding relationships among different living things.

glands
Organs in the body that produce chemicals used by other parts of the body.

isolated
Set apart from the rest.

species
A group of animals or plants that are alike and can breed with one another.

taste aversion
Tending to avoid a food because of a past bad experience eating that food.

TO LEARN MORE

BOOKS

Amstutz, Lisa J. *Invasive Species*. Minneapolis: Abdo Publishing, 2018.

Gilles, Renae. *Invasive Species in Infographics*. Ann Arbor, MI: Cherry Lake Publishing, 2021.

Wilcox, Merrie-Ellen. *Nature Out of Balance: How Invasive Species Are Changing the Planet*. Custer, WA: Orca Book Publishers, 2021.

NOTE TO EDUCATORS

Visit **www.focusreaders.com** to find lesson plans, activities, links, and other resources related to this title.

INDEX

Answer Key: 1. Answers will vary; **2.** Answers will vary; **3.** A; **4.** B